cntre space

cntre space

MALIKA IMAD WARDA

RESOURCE *Publications* • Eugene, Oregon

CNTRE SPACE

Copyright © 2018 Malika Imad Warda. All rights reserved. Except for brief quotations in critical publications or reviews, no part of this book may be reproduced in any manner without prior written permission from the publisher. Write: Permissions, Wipf and Stock Publishers, 199 W. 8th Ave., Suite 3, Eugene, OR 97401.

Resource Publications
An Imprint of Wipf and Stock Publishers
199 W. 8th Ave., Suite 3
Eugene, OR 97401

www.wipfandstock.com

PAPERBACK ISBN: 978-1-5326-6474-8
HARDCOVER ISBN: 978-1-5326-6475-5
EBOOK ISBN: 978-1-5326-6476-2

Manufactured in the U.S.A.   12/07/18

dedicated to the evolution of our spirit

the space in which all beings meet

cntre space

as each lover
surrenders
to the other
they forget
who it is
they are,
their only task
is to be
the space
for their
other half,
and neither
lover
sees
the other
for this is
who they
are

I'll sing
to the hymns
that rise
within

even thoughts
are heard;
they add to her complexity
such responsibility
bestowed upon us all
as we shape our destiny.
from her womb
all has come
to be
so we dance
sing
and breathe,
and all shall remain
in the fabric
of forever,
molding the way
for all who play
the game

although unreachable
she is known
to all
who look within

now
let everything work,
to open,
to scratch,
and chip away
at all that you
accumulated
along the way

freedom is not our human potential;
freedom is the essence of all,
not to be sought after,
not to be viewed
as anything other
than what you are,
freedom is never lost
nor is it gained,
there is no choice in the matter,
freedom is all that there is
and whether you believe it or not
is irrelevant
for freedom knows not

his silence set him free

I offer myself
so that you
may be,
I will die
every moment
and let you
breathe,
over and over
I'll set you free,
for the truth of me
there is no such thing,
so say not I,
nor her,
or him,
this will only cause
your
suffering

transparent
flesh and bone
my heart
is known

you cease to be anything other than
whole and complete;
you are free
beyond all limitations

his word
marks the heart
that beats in all

stories
upon
stories
of your glory

truth exists
to all who
open their hearts
to the authority
of his presence
and allow his love
to open you up
in ways you never knew,
a love so pure
and unforgiving
it may show
as the dark night
of the soul
unearthing debris
from old worlds
running loops
that cripple,
and so that is why
one must surrender
fearlessly
into his embrace
for sometimes
we cannot see
that which
we cannot see

and all that you are
is the deepest truth
that lights up existence;
the deepest love
that you may never know
because you are

exhausted
the child shuts his eyes
and for the first time
he sleeps all night
in the ease of his surrender

you infuse me
with the sweetest
nectar

he runs wild
in the vastness
of his own
presence,
and trusts
in the power
of his being
to show him
the way
to freely express
the forever evolving
radiance
that is
his truth,
and every moment
that unfolds
in the wake
of his acceptance
is the pure
and raw
love
that commands
nothing
for he is
everything

it was freedom
that had me prisoned
for there is nowhere to hide
when he who looks up
so too
looks down

through Gods grace
we relearn
who it is we are,
ever so slowly
reclaiming ourselves
through the shedding
of false identity;
a perfect set of conditions
in which we were gifted
as a means
of self-discovery,
forged over so many lifetimes,
and all that is here now
belongs to no one,
for if you take hold
of any such thing
you do so at your own risk,
succumbing to localized points
on a map
that point to nowhere,
and yet everywhere

freedom is an expression of
absolute absorption
followed by sweet surrender
—climax

may we all swim freely

poisoned
by our over consumption
we suffered
and grew
we wore every single facet;
the garment
became our truth

all that once was
fuels the fire
that burns inside,
enriching creation,
expression,
experience,
and all that emerges
in the perfection of now
is merely a continuation
and fertilization
of her eternal dance

we all breathe
for the same cause,
for the breath
knows no preference,
instead she serves
as an extension
of his dream

unrestricted
the field is endless
and she worries not,
calm
among the
uncertainty,
she thrives in depths
further out;
complexity,
intensity,
detail,
fading in and out,
feeding herself
off herself,
fueling possibility
infinitely,
sleepless,
boundless,
thoughtless,
she is alone;
wastes not,
wants not,
a user
because she sees herself
in all

it's all just singular awareness
no matter how *we* look at it

with eyes fixated
you limit your field
to a single possibility
in an infinite world

only through your power
can we rise beyond identification
and the illusion of individual worth
for in an instant
you shatter
every concept held dear
as you spread far and wide
rejoicing,
your freedom is uncontainable
for you are heaven
and you weep from above
endless tears of light
that manifest
and reflect back to you
my love

one must die
a conscious death
to truly know
what it is
to live

through the death of me
I came to be

it all
began
to change

over
and over
again

one thing
stayed
the same

in love
we
remained

look around
with softness in your eyes
so that all becomes
undisguised

fear and doubt
might cloud our view
but love
is
our only truth

we're singing love into existence
in the name of the Lord

everything flows
in and out,
in and out
in unison
with his heartbeat,
no pause
to catch his breath,
or to dissect
the nature of
the dance,
for this would cause
the seas to part,
and that which sustains all
does so entirely,
for eternity,
as infinite love,
and that is all

a single truth;
the cause
of every
possibility

as she disperses;
the universe made,
and although she plays
she remains backstage;
she exists among her children
as all the forms of grace,
she knows the game,
the suffering her being undertakes,
only in the mind of the other,
she breathes it all into existence
to feel it all,
as her children do,
she is the dream she creates
to participate,
aware of the sacrifice made,
for her revelation dawns
in infinite ways

I let you mold
this life I hold

you are your own truth
and that is all

let me drown from the weight of your love
so I no longer beg for your mercy,
so I no longer cry out your name,
dissolve me entirely
so that only you remain

self-love
is the intimacy
one experiences
at the inmost depths
of themselves

this is for you;
all of it is,
not because you say so
but because you are so,
not because you are greater than
but because you are,
for all manifestations are you,
and you too
rest alone,
not by yourself,
but as you are;
known,
unknown,
but this means nothing to you
for you just are

weightless
is the love we share
and the heaviest
burden
I bare

the One exists
as the formless undercurrent
of all there ever is,
giving birth to infinite possibilities
and yet remains unchanged,
the creator is the created,
and yet he sees no difference,
for all is his very nature,
he is God;
the alpha and the omega,
everything and nothing,
not by separation,
but as he is

she marvels at the splendor
emerging out of
and back into
as all things do

we only see
to the extent
of our openness,
and he who resists nothing
lives in paradise for eternity

a subtle current
climbs its way up,
it forces my surrender
and begs to dominate,
in all the different ways
I came
over and over again
to the rhythm
of a single breath,
a single heartbeat;
the pulse of creation,
I lost myself
with no end,
again
and
again,
I came

the strength it takes
to break

through the veils of time and space
remnants of the past
emerge from your depths
playing sweet tunes
of memory,
of life and death and rebirth

non attachment is
understanding
the relative nature
of all things

*it's all just a matter of
our state of being*

as one looks upon
her delicate dance
she too
sees you,
is it that every action
affects her reaction
or does her body serve
as the cause for all display

I ask that you expose
the dreams I hold deep inside;
may you fill these places
with new dreams
of your nature
I wish to make known

beyond the manifest
she simultaneously thrives freely
as the Source of all

there is nothing
that cannot
bring us
to God

to deny any experience
is to deny God

just lose yourself baby-
you're already free

everything has already happened
and *here*
you have always been
—*Timelessness*

nirvana;
continuous renewal,
independent,
free,
and yet contained
by its own existence,
endlessly arising
out of itself,
celebrating
its glory,
infinitely uplifting
its own potential,
nothing stops its flow
for it is boundless
and knows nothing else

when she wants out
she will move
with great force,
no matter how hard
you tried
to keep it all together,
she will annihilate
every last thread
so that she may live
her fullest potential
however she requires
for maximum expansion

as worlds unravel
her truth be known

freedom is an inner expression of the heart
that knows no bounds

who am I?
who am I?
who am I?
who am I?
who am I?
who am I?
who am I?
who am I?
who am I?
who am I?
who am I?
who am I?
who am I?
who am I?
who am I?

who am I?
who am I?
who am I?
who am I?
who am I?
who am I?
who am I?
who am I?
who am I?
who am I?
who am I?
who am I?
who am I?
who am I?
who am I?

we never really get to heaven
just to deeper
and broader states
of our heavenly being

only love
remained
we were
together in
always
forever in
here
there
everywhere
love was
love is
all there
ever is
this day
yesterday
and every
other day
it remains
the same
nothing more
nothing less

don't ask for a miracle
of your preference
for you fail to believe
and you do not see

my path is simple,
for wherever I turn
God is there

our path lies not
in a particular direction
but in knowing
that we have already arrived,
and it matters not which road we travel,
all are holy,
for all the markings of grace
point the way

happiness is
the dawning
of Spirit

I was weightless in heaven
with my feet on the earth

she welcomes all such form,
for the light,
the dark,
and everything in between
is the embodiment of possibility
and she says yes to it all

let it be our mission
to *learn* to listen
to thy inner wisdom
—Meditation

it all just comes and goes,
existing
as the ever-changing miracle
that is life,
and he knows of its temporary nature,
which is why
he will always let it be,
for never again
will it ever be

within each of us
lies the ultimate psychedelic trip

by being here now
we honor the sacred truth
of our eternal flame,
by being here now
we participate wholeheartedly
in nature's dance,
by being here now
we experience the gift of life;
of spontaneity
and change
that emanates from the rootedness
and permanence of now

more and more
I realize
I know nothing
and never
have I felt
so free

we are a single Source
experiencing
every dimension
of our multi-faceted nature.
there is no greater or lesser experience,
just a single moment in time

keep softening into the experience
so that you may become
the most effortless
and concentrated
expression
of the very moment
that is
all that you are

your presence
softens the uncertainty
of our singularity

I have the role of many
as I am
of which I'm not any
but to you I am
what I am

my eyes speak the truth of my heart
for they only ever look within

and I know
all which I see
is purely a reflection
of the God in me

all that I am
is the calm
for the storm

when the mind is
empty
the possibilities are
endless,
for here
who's
to say

from the comfort of Mother Earth
I look to Father God,
filled by their presence,
I am love
glorious love

there is nothing that is ever happening to us;
we live through it all
unaffected

you are the Self;
the shapeless shape
of many,
you are not any

peace is not a state
of mind,
it is a state
of Being,
in love
with
God

to be in love
is to simply
Be

you're only ever
here

wisdom is
old news
informing itself
through new
medium

true authentic self-expression is
a pure stream
of consciousness;
a statement of
our highest truth

love is ever present

love is wild;
it's fierce and unforgiving,
it's the spiraling out of control,
it's freedom itself,
it's our power
untamed

happiness is realized
in the perfection of now.
we need not strive for happiness
just stillness

does birth not take place
the moment of
conception.
do we ever really
leave
the Mothers womb

the individual
is he
who sees himself
in all,
for him
there is no difference,
no separation,
all is the expression
of his own heart

these words are still just
a desperate attempt
to hold on

let go

open mindedness
is a state
of non-judgmental
acceptance
that is far beyond
the mind itself

the offering of love
is made possible
only when love itself
has transformed the individual
who then realizes
love is not an exchange
but is in fact
the abundant flow
of life itself;
the Source of consciousness,
that is entirely free of all else.
there is nothing to give
and nothing to receive
for who is there
but love itself.

love is all that there is

love is limited
by its own
limitlessness

in Samadhi
I found he
who breathes
immortality
into me

love is all that you are
when you are not there

love is absolute
always and forever

love knows not
for love only ever is

dying
into
existence

there was never
any body
there was never
anybody

choice is not
a man free
for choice is
nothing but duality
in his mind you see,
but free is he
who sees
the Almighty
in everything

unafraid but still weighed
by the lives lived
and lived
to this day,
and I've survived
time and time
the lives I've lived
not left behind,
and the soul still shines
through the binds
of the many lives
and the clouded mind
with silent cries
to rectify

no man can ever be enlightened,
for enlightenment is
where man
is not

you have to die
to get to heaven

and as we wake in the morning
let us not forget
the night we spent together,
we became the night together,
naked in our slumber,
we made love as one another,
as lovers with no name

let your words
sing of the life force
that runs through you,
let them speak
of the energy
that vibrates and ripples
through every cell
of your being,
let the rhythm of life, of nature,
express itself
in all its glory,
as it continuously unearths itself,
let her power shake you,
break you,
and remake you
over and over again

you are indescribable
power way beyond perception,
your magic shows
in every way
seen and unseen,
life is a celebration
of your very real existence,
you were never born
for you have always been
far beyond this dream

soaking in the ocean
of my very own existence,
the essence of my heart,
the fullness of
your grace

game
over

you
have
arrived

now
please
continue

prayer

let yourself be soft
and know that you are ok
eyes closed
heart is open to the subtle rhythm
of breath
gentle gaze rests upon the ocean that stands before
where unveiling currents pour fourth
you are being fed and deeply nourished
infused with the most potent flavors
in this magnetic communion with the divine
nothing needs to be done
just soften
soften into the natural unfolding
into the everlasting body of acceptance
of undying love
let it move freely through you
until there is nothing else

www.ingramcontent.com/pod-product-compliance
Lightning Source LLC
Chambersburg PA
CBHW070504090426
42735CB00012B/2668